ALEX
KUSKOWSKI

A FUN AND CREATIVE INTRODUCTION TO FIBER ART

COOL

CROCHETING

for KIDS

Checkerboard
Library

An Imprint of Abdo Publishing
www.abdopublishing.com

VISIT US AT WWW.ABDOPUBLISHING.COM

Published by Abdo Publishing, a division of ABDO, PO Box 398166, Minneapolis, Minnesota 55439. Copyright © 2015 by Abdo Consulting Group, Inc. International copyrights reserved in all countries. No part of this book may be reproduced in any form without written permission from the publisher. Checkerboard Library™ is a trademark and logo of Abdo Publishing.

Printed in the United States of America, North Mankato, Minnesota
062014
092014

THIS BOOK CONTAINS
RECYCLED MATERIALS

Design and Production: Anders Hanson, Mighty Media, Inc.
Series Editor: Liz Salzmann
Photo Credits: Anders Hanson, Shutterstock

The following manufacturers/names appearing in this book are trademarks: Susan Bates®

Library of Congress Cataloging-in-Publication Data
Kuskowski, Alex., author.
  Cool crocheting for kids : a fun and creative introduction to fiber art / Alex Kuskowski.
     pages cm. -- (Cool fiber art)
  Audience: Ages 8-10.
  Includes bibliographical references and index.
  ISBN 978-1-62403-306-3 (alk. paper)
  1. Crocheting--Juvenile literature. I. Title.
  TT820.K87 2015
  746.43'4--dc23
                          2013043073

TO ADULT HELPERS

This is your chance to assist someone new to crafting! As children learn to craft they develop new skills, gain confidence, and make cool things. These activities are designed to help children learn how to make their own craft projects. Some activities may need more assistance than others. Be there to offer guidance when they need it. Encourage them to do as much as they can on their own. Be a cheerleader for their creativity.

Before getting started, remember to lay down ground rules for using the crafting tools and cleaning up. There should always be adult supervision when a child uses a sharp tool.

TABLE OF CONTENTS

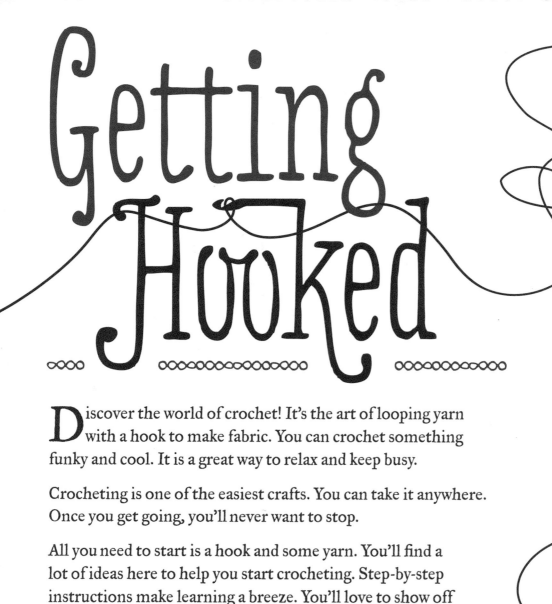

Getting Hooked

Discover the world of crochet! It's the art of looping yarn with a hook to make fabric. You can crochet something funky and cool. It is a great way to relax and keep busy.

Crocheting is one of the easiest crafts. You can take it anywhere. Once you get going, you'll never want to stop.

All you need to start is a hook and some yarn. You'll find a lot of ideas here to help you start crocheting. Step-by-step instructions make learning a breeze. You'll love to show off the things you make. Just turn the page and get hooked!

❧ Tools *of the* Trade ❧

CROCHET HOOK

You only need one hook to get started. Hooks come in different sizes. They are made out of wood, plastic, or **aluminum**.

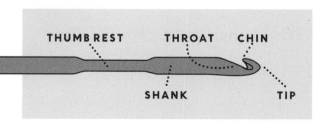

THUMB REST   THROAT   CHIN

SHANK   TIP

HOOK SIZES

Make sure to use the right size hook. Many **patterns** offer suggestions on what size to use. See the chart to find out how they relate to one another.

SIZE NUMBER	METRIC SIZE (MM)	US SIZE
1	2.25	B/1
2	2.75	C/2
3	3.25	D/3
4	3.5	E/4
5	3.75	F/5
6	4–4.25	G/6
7	4.5	7
8	5	H/8
9	5.5	I/9
10	6	J/10
11	6.5	K/10.5
12	8	L/11
13	9	M/13

YARN

Yarn is the main material used in crochet. It has many sizes, weights, and shapes. You can also crochet with string and wire.

NATURAL FIBER

SYNTHETIC FIBER

YARN FIBER

Yarn can be made with natural fibers or synthetic fibers. Natural fibers come from animals and plants, such as sheep and cotton. Synthetic fibers are man-made fibers, such as acrylic or nylon.

STARTING UP

**GET GOING WITH
THESE DIRECTIONS!**

WHAT YOU NEED

**WORSTED (#4) YARN,
J (6MM) HOOK**

START WITH A SLIPKNOT

1 Let the yarn tail hang in front of your left palm. Wrap the yarn loosely around your first two fingers.

2 Pull the yarn forward between your second and third fingers. Push it up through the yarn over your fingers so it makes a loop.

3 Hold both ends of the yarn in your left hand. Hold the loop in your right hand. Pull it snug. Put the loop on the crochet hook. Pull on the ends to tighten the loop.

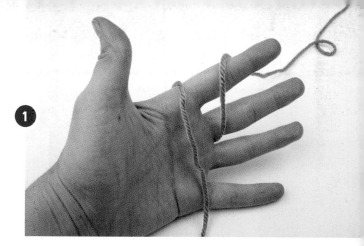

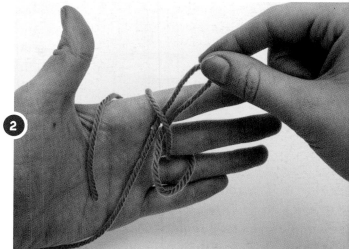

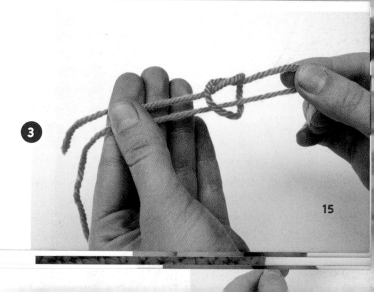

15

CROCHET-A-CARD

HANDMADE WITH LOVE!

WHAT YOU NEED

CARD STOCK, ¼-INCH
HOLE PUNCH, YARN
(#3 OR LESS), G (#6)
HOOK, RULER, SCISSORS,
DECORATIONS, GLUE

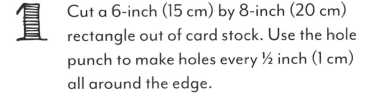

1. Cut a 6-inch (15 cm) by 8-inch (20 cm) rectangle out of card stock. Use the hole punch to make holes every ½ inch (1 cm) all around the edge.

2. Make a slipknot and put the loop on the hook. Stick the hook through a corner hole. Yarn over around the paper. Pull the yarn through the hole. Then pull the yarn through the slipknot loop.

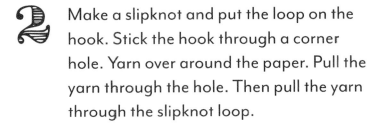

3. Chain 3. Put the hook through the next hole. Yarn over around the paper. Pull the yarn through the hole and the loop on the hook.

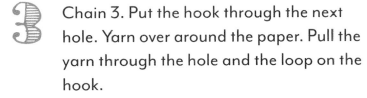

4. Repeat step 3 until you get to the next corner. At the corner, crochet two stitches in one hole.

5. Repeat steps 3 and 4 until all the holes are filled. Cut the yarn. Thread the tail of the slipknot through the loop. Tie a knot. Cut off the ends.

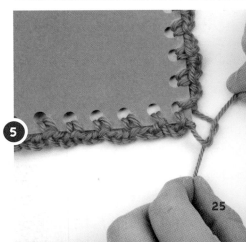

6. Fold the card in half. Add decorations.

25